COM and .NET Synergy

Mastering Component Object Model Integration for Robust Windows Applications

Violet Roman

Contents

1 Introduction to COM and .NET

The Component Object Model (COM) represents a significant milestone in software development, enabling reusable components to communicate across different programming languages and applications. Its architecture, based on interfaces and binary standards, allows for flexibility and interoperability unlike anything seen before. Understanding COM's core concepts, such as interfaces, reference counting, and marshaling, is fundamental for anyone aiming to master its integration with .NET. Grasping these concepts forms the bedrock upon which more advanced techniques are built. It's essential to remember that COM is not just a technology; it's a paradigm shift in how we think about software modularity and reusability.

The .NET Framework, a powerful and versatile platform from Microsoft, provides a rich environment for building various applications. Its common language runtime (CLR) manages memory, handles exceptions, and ensures type safety, offering a significant advantage over traditional COM development. Yet, the beauty of .NET lies in its ability to seamlessly interact with existing COM components, leveraging the strengths of both worlds. This interoperability allows .NET developers to utilize pre-existing COM libraries and integrate them into their applications. This interaction doesn't require rewriting existing code, significantly reducing development time and effort. Mastering this interaction unlocks a universe of possibilities.

Early binding offers a performance advantage due to compile-time type checking. It is the optimal approach for utilizing COM components where performance is critical. The compiler can verify type compatibility, eliminating runtime type errors and generating efficient native code. However, early binding demands referencing COM type libraries explicitly, which might limit flexibility in dealing with evolving COM components. Late binding, on the other hand, relies on runtime type discovery, hence it is beneficial when dealing with components whose types are unknown at compile time. Though less efficient, it offers flexibility and enables dynamic interactions. The choice between these two methods depends on the specific requirements of your application.

Understanding how data is marshaled between COM and .NET is crucial. Marshalling involves the conversion of data structures between different memory spaces and data types. Understanding this process is vital in preventing errors and ensuring seamless data transfer between the two environments. For example, strings may require different encoding conversions, and object references need careful management to avoid memory leaks. Failure to properly handle marshaling can result in unexpected crashes, data corruption, and application instability. In-depth knowledge of this aspect of COM interop is therefore essential.

Error handling is paramount when working with COM components in .NET. Since components are often built by different vendors and have diverse error reporting mechanisms, robust error handling prevents application crashes and ensures graceful failure. Implement structured exception handling using try-catch blocks to intercept and handle exceptions from COM calls. It is important to translate COM errors into .NET exceptions for better consistency with the .NET error-handling model. Remember, anticipate potential problems and carefully handle them to ensure your application's stability and robustness.

Building COM components requires a well-defined structure and a thorough understanding of interfaces. Interfaces define the contract between the component and its consumers, ensuring consistency and preventing unexpected behavior. Properly designed interfaces should be cohesive and promote reusability. Implementing these interfaces in a well-structured and organized fashion is critical. During the development process, rigorously test each component's functionality to ensure reliable operation within its defined specifications. Thorough testing is key to preventing issues later in the software lifecycle. Deployment of COM components involves registration in the Windows registry, which maps component interfaces to their implementation. Understanding the registry entries necessary for proper component recognition is critical. Correct deployment ensures seamless component integration in the target system. Deployment mistakes can cause component load failures and various runtime errors. Mastering this aspect of COM development is essential for successful component integration and utilization across various applications. Appropriate versioning strategies must be implemented to maintain compatibility with previous versions and to enable easy updates and upgrades.

Security considerations are significant when integrating COM components into .NET applications. Unsecured components can introduce vulnerabilities, potentially compromising the entire system. Implement security best practices, such as access control lists and secure code handling, to minimize risks. It's crucial to treat COM components as potentially untrusted entities. A multi-layered security approach offers the best protection against various potential threats.

Finally, remember that COM and .NET offer powerful tools for building complex and robust applications. Their synergy provides flexibility, interoperability, and reusability that simplifies software development. By understanding the fundamental concepts of COM, mastering .NET interoperability, and implementing robust error handling and security measures, you can confidently leverage this technology to develop high-quality, scalable, and secure Windows applications. The journey may seem daunting at times, but the rewards are well worth the effort.

1.1 COM Fundamentals

The Component Object Model, or COM, is a binary standard. It's not just a set of libraries; it's a specification that dictates how software components interact. Think of it as a contract—if you build a component adhering to the COM rules, it can seamlessly work with other COM-compliant components, regardless of programming language or even the operating system version. This interoperability is COM's greatest strength. Understanding this fundamental principle unlocks the power of reusable software building blocks.

COM relies heavily on interfaces. These interfaces define the contracts between components, specifying precisely what methods and properties are available. When a component implements an interface, it promises to provide the functionality outlined in that interface. Another component can then use that interface to interact with it, without needing to know the internal workings of the first component. This abstraction is crucial for modularity and maintainability, preventing components from becoming overly entangled.

One of the most important aspects of COM is its reliance on binary compatibility. Unlike many other technologies that depend on source code compatibility, COM's binary nature simplifies the integration process. A COM component compiled for one system can often work without modification on others. This is because the interface definitions—which are binary contracts—remain consistent. This dramatically simplifies deployment, reducing the likelihood of compatibility issues arising between different systems or versions.

COM components are registered in the system registry. This registry entry acts as a directory, allowing applications to locate and load the necessary components at runtime. The registry holds details such as the component's class ID (CLSID), which serves as a unique identifier, and the path to the component's executable file. This mechanism, while powerful, can sometimes be a source of difficulties, especially when dealing with multiple versions of the same component. Careful management of registry entries is therefore a vital aspect of successful COM development.

However, COM's reliance on the registry isn't without drawbacks. Incorrect registration can lead to runtime errors, and managing registry entries manually can be tedious. Tools exist to aid in this process, but understanding the fundamentals remains essential. Moreover, the registry's hierarchical structure can become quite complex, and navigating it to find and troubleshoot issues requires a methodical and patient approach. This is why many prefer using newer methods for registering components.

Marshalling, the process of converting data between different memory spaces, is crucial for inter-process communication. When COM components interact, they might be running in different processes or even on different machines. Marshalling handles the complexities of moving data between these contexts, ensuring its integrity and compatibility. The different marshalling mechanisms available, each with varying performance characteristics, have to be carefully chosen to suit each situation.

One could also think about error handling within the COM environment. Robust error handling is particularly important in a distributed system where components might fail independently. COM uses exceptions to signal errors, and proper error handling should be integrated into all components to prevent cascading failures. This includes not only catching exceptions, but also implementing strategies for graceful degradation or recovery in case of errors. It's crucial that your application can not only detect but handle them with a high degree of efficiency.

Understanding these core tenets—interfaces, binary compatibility, registry-based registration, marshalling, and error handling—is crucial for building and using COM components effectively. This foundation lays the groundwork for more advanced COM topics, allowing you to create robust and reusable software components for Windows applications. Mastering these fundamentals is the key to unlocking the full potential of COM, providing a strong base for your journey into the world of COM and .NET integration. Remember that while the registry can sometimes cause issues, proper understanding and careful management are crucial to success in using COM.

1.2 .NET Framework Overview

The .NET Framework, a cornerstone of Microsoft's Windows development ecosystem, provides a robust and versatile platform for building a wide range of applications. It's a managed execution environment, meaning the framework itself handles memory management and other low-level details, freeing developers to focus on application logic. This significantly reduces the risk of memory leaks and other common programming errors. Its extensive class library, the Framework Class Library (FCL), provides ready-made components for almost every conceivable task, from simple string manipulation to complex network communications. This dramatically accelerates development, leading to faster time-to-market for applications.

Understanding the Common Language Runtime (CLR), the heart of the .NET Framework, is crucial. The CLR manages the execution of .NET code, providing services such as garbage collection, exception handling, and security. It ensures that code runs reliably and securely, regardless of the programming language used. Think of the CLR as a sophisticated virtual machine, translating your code into machine-understandable instructions while managing resources efficiently. This consistent environment allows for seamless interoperability between different .NET languages, a key benefit for large projects involving multiple developers or legacy code integration.

A crucial aspect of the .NET Framework is its support for different programming languages. While C\section{is often the language of choice, the framework is language-agnostic. Languages like VB.NET, F#, and even some others can be used to build applications that run seamlessly within the .NET environment. This language interoperability promotes flexibility and allows developers to select the language best suited to their skills and the specific task at hand. This isn't just about syntax; it's about leveraging the strengths of each language to build efficient and maintainable software.}

The .NET Framework's architecture is layered, providing a clear separation of concerns. At the base sits the CLR, managing the execution of code. Above it lies the FCL, a vast collection of classes and interfaces offering pre-built functionality. Developers build their applications on top of the FCL, leveraging its components to create powerful and feature-rich software. This modular design promotes code reusability and reduces development time significantly. Each layer interacts efficiently, providing a solid foundation for building robust applications, and simplifies debugging and maintenance due to this organized structure.

One of the significant advantages of .NET is its strong support for building Windows Forms and WPF applications. Windows Forms provides a straightforward way to create classic desktop applications with a familiar look and feel, while WPF (Windows Presentation Foundation) offers a more modern and flexible approach to user interface design, enabling the creation of visually rich and interactive applications. Both technologies integrate seamlessly with the .NET Framework, providing developers with a full range of options for creating compelling user experiences. The choice often depends on project requirements and the complexity of the user interface.

Furthermore, ASP.NET, a web application framework built on the .NET Framework, allows developers to create dynamic and scalable websites. ASP.NET MVC (Model-View-Controller) offers a structured approach to web development, separating concerns for improved maintainability and testability. Web Forms, a more traditional approach, offers a faster way to develop web applications for simple projects. The framework provides robust security features, database integration capabilities and easy deployment options, making it a strong platform for web development regardless of the method chosen.

Beyond its capabilities for creating standalone applications, the .NET Framework shines in its ability to integrate with other technologies. The framework's strong interoperability features, notably COM interop, are crucial for bridging the gap between legacy systems and modern .NET applications. This interoperability extends to databases, allowing for seamless integration with various data sources. This allows businesses to leverage existing investments while still benefiting from the advantages of the .NET Framework, leading to cost savings and more efficient workflows. For instance, integrating older COM components into a new .NET application enhances efficiency and avoids the substantial cost of rewriting the older software.

.NET's extensive documentation and a large, active community offer substantial support for developers. Countless online resources, tutorials, and forums provide answers to common questions, and readily available examples streamline the learning curve. This robust support system ensures that developers can quickly find solutions to problems and efficiently use the framework. This accessible knowledge base significantly benefits beginners and seasoned developers alike, facilitating ongoing learning and professional development.

In conclusion, the .NET Framework provides a comprehensive and powerful platform for building robust Windows applications, combining managed code execution, an extensive class library, and strong interoperability with other technologies. Its support for multiple languages, diverse application types, and a vibrant community makes it a highly valuable tool for any developer aiming to create high-quality, maintainable, and efficient software. The framework, in essence, simplifies complexities, thus freeing up developers to focus on innovation and building effective and user-friendly solutions. The rich set of features allows the user to create diverse applications, both simple and complex ones. Understanding its core components and capabilities is therefore essential for anyone serious about Windows application development, especially when considering its synergy with COM.

2 COM Interop Basics

Understanding COM interoperability is fundamental to leveraging the power of both COM and .NET. It's about bridging the gap between two distinct, yet complementary, worlds—allowing .NET applications to seamlessly interact with legacy COM components and vice-versa. This synergy opens up access to a vast library of existing components, saving significant development time and resources. Think of it as unlocking a treasure trove of pre-built functionalities. Imagine needing a specific cryptographic function; a well-established COM component might already provide it, ready for immediate use within your .NET project. The key to accessing this wealth lies in mastering the principles of interoperability.

Data marshalling is the critical process of translating data between COM and .NET environments. These two platforms often represent data differently. For example, a COM component might use BSTR (Basic String) for strings, whereas .NET utilizes its own string type. Marshalling seamlessly handles these conversions, ensuring that data is correctly passed between the two worlds without causing compatibility errors. Without proper marshalling, you'll encounter crashes, unexpected behavior, and frustrating debugging sessions. Understanding the intricacies of how this process works is crucial for building robust and reliable applications. It involves a deep understanding of data types, memory management and the subtle differences in how each environment structures information. Failure to properly manage this aspect can lead to memory leaks and data corruption.

Error handling is paramount in any software development endeavor, especially when dealing with interoperability. Errors can originate from either the COM component, the .NET application, or even the marshalling process itself. Effective error handling ensures that your application doesn't crash or produce unpredictable results. A critical technique is using structured exception handling (try-catch blocks in .NET) to gracefully handle potential errors, providing informative error messages and preventing application failures. This approach is indispensable for creating user-friendly and dependable applications. Consider scenarios where a COM component fails due to network issues or a file access problem. Your .NET application needs a way to detect these errors, inform the user appropriately, and recover gracefully, preventing a cascade of errors. Robust error handling is more than just catching exceptions; it is about designing your application to anticipate failure points and respond intelligently.

Working with COM interfaces requires a clear understanding of their role in the interoperability process. Interfaces define the contract between the COM component and the .NET application. They specify the methods and properties that the COM component exposes. Properly using these interfaces ensures a clear and unambiguous communication pathway. Think of an interface as a contract—both the COM component and the .NET client must adhere to it. Ignoring this contract leads to runtime errors and unpredictable results. You must accurately map the interface methods and properties to your .NET code, paying close attention to data types and parameter passing conventions. Each method call must be precisely coordinated to avoid type mismatches and unexpected behavior. Careful planning and a thorough understanding of the interface definition are essential to successful COM interop.

Finally, the choice between early and late binding significantly impacts how your .NET application interacts with COM components. Early binding, utilizing type libraries, offers compile-time type checking, improving code quality and reducing runtime errors. Late binding, on the other hand, provides more flexibility, but at the cost of runtime performance and the possibility of errors that only surface at run time. The decision of which to use depends on the specific requirements of your application. Early binding allows the compiler to verify the compatibility of your calls, leading to fewer unexpected runtime surprises. It's generally preferred for applications where stability and performance are critical. Late binding's greater flexibility allows for more dynamic interactions, valuable in scenarios where the exact COM component isn't known at compile time. The best choice hinges on the balance between development speed, performance, and the risk tolerance of your application's behavior. Consider the trade-offs carefully before making a decision that will impact your application's robustness and efficiency.

2.1 Understanding Interop

Understanding the intricacies of COM interop is crucial for anyone aiming to seamlessly integrate COM components into their .NET applications. It's about bridging the gap between two distinct but powerful worlds, leveraging the strengths of each. This requires a deep understanding of how data is exchanged, how errors are handled, and ultimately, how to manage the entire process efficiently and robustly.

The fundamental principle lies in recognizing the differences. COM, with its emphasis on binary compatibility and interface-based programming, operates fundamentally differently from the managed code environment of .NET. Understanding this core distinction is paramount. Think of it like trying to connect two different types of plumbing systems – you need the right adapters and careful planning to ensure a smooth flow.

Successfully navigating COM interop requires mastering the art of marshaling. This isn't just about data conversion; it's about ensuring data is correctly represented and accessed across the interoperability boundary. Consider different data types, their memory representation, and how they're handled by each environment. For example, a simple string in .NET might require a more complex representation in COM, and vice versa. Failure to properly marshal data will result in runtime errors, data corruption, or even application crashes.

Error handling forms the bedrock of any robust interop solution. Exceptions raised within a COM component need to be gracefully handled by your .NET application. Conversely, errors originating within the .NET code must be reported back to the COM component in a way that maintains system stability. The methods for this vary widely depending on your chosen approach; therefore, careful consideration of your error handling mechanisms is crucial. Failing to implement proper error handling mechanisms might lead to unexpected and potentially catastrophic failures within your applications.

Furthermore, the choice between early and late binding influences how you interact with COM components. Early binding, leveraging type libraries, offers stronger type checking and compile-time error detection, resulting in more robust code. However, late binding provides flexibility, allowing you to interact with components dynamically at runtime. This flexibility is advantageous when dealing with components whose type libraries aren't readily available or when you need to adapt to unforeseen changes. Your selection will be determined by factors like the stability of your COM components and the need for dynamism.

Remember, performance is a critical concern. Inefficient interop can severely impact the responsiveness and overall performance of your application. Factors such as data marshaling overhead and the frequency of cross-boundary calls directly affect performance. Optimizing your interop strategy by minimizing data transfers, using efficient data structures and leveraging techniques such as asynchronous calls, can greatly enhance performance. Neglecting performance considerations can lead to sluggish applications that negatively impact the user experience.

Beyond the technical aspects, consider the practical implications. Versioning your COM components and ensuring compatibility with different .NET versions are critical for long-term maintainability. Without careful planning, you risk encountering compatibility issues and requiring extensive rework. This forward-thinking approach ensures the longevity and stability of your application. A well-structured versioning strategy, therefore, is paramount in the development process.

In conclusion, mastering COM interop requires a multifaceted approach. It's not simply about connecting two systems; it's about understanding their fundamental differences, leveraging the strengths of both, and carefully managing data exchange, error handling, and overall performance. The reward, however, is the ability to seamlessly integrate the functionality of powerful COM components into your .NET applications, creating robust and efficient solutions. Therefore, dedicate the necessary time and effort to understand each aspect, and you'll be well-equipped to navigate the complexities of COM interop. The result will be a more robust and maintainable software product.

2.2 Marshalling Data

Efficient data marshalling is paramount for seamless COM and .NET interaction. Imagine trying to send a complex object, like a custom data structure, across the interoperability boundary; without proper marshalling, you'll encounter errors. The underlying mechanisms, often hidden from the developer, handle the conversion of data types between the COM and .NET environments. This conversion process isn't always straightforward; different data types, memory management schemes, and object models can cause conflicts if not handled expertly. Understanding these underlying processes allows developers to anticipate potential issues. Effective solutions require a good grasp of the mechanics involved. This goes beyond simple data types; it encompasses more complex scenarios, including custom classes and interfaces.

Choosing the right marshalling mechanism is critical. The default marshalling behavior might suffice for simple types. However, when dealing with more complex data structures, such as arrays or custom classes containing nested objects, you might need to implement custom marshalling strategies. This allows finer control over the conversion process and improves performance and stability. Utilizing attributes, particularly within your COM component's interfaces, provides explicit direction on how your data should be marshaled, leaving no ambiguity. Carefully consider the implications of choosing specific attributes. Improperly used attributes can lead to unexpected results, including memory leaks or data corruption. Remember, careful planning and thoughtful implementation are key to success in marshaling data effectively.

The importance of understanding the different marshalling strategies cannot be overstated. One strategy might be perfectly suitable for one situation but lead to instability in another. The choice depends on many factors including the type and complexity of the data being marshalled, performance requirements, and security considerations. For instance, using a simpler, less resource-intensive approach for frequently marshaled data may be preferable to a more complex, robust method for less frequent transfers. This optimization process involves evaluating trade-offs between efficiency and stability. In-depth knowledge of these tradeoffs will allow the developer to implement the best possible solution for each scenario.

Debugging problems related to data marshalling can be challenging. Errors often manifest unexpectedly, possibly far removed from their source. Using debugging tools is invaluable. These tools allow tracing data flow and identifying points of failure. Pay attention to the details. Many problems stem from subtle inconsistencies in data types or attribute mismatches between the COM component and the .NET application. Careful examination of your code, tracing through the process, and thorough testing are essential for isolating and resolving these problems. Remember to approach troubleshooting methodically, identifying the problem's root cause rather than merely treating the symptoms.

Consider the impact of performance. Inefficient marshalling can drastically slow down your application. Analyzing your code, identifying potential bottlenecks, and adopting optimizations based on your testing results will often yield significant performance improvements. Remember that the size of the data being marshalled has a substantial impact on performance. Minimizing the amount of data transferred across the boundary, choosing the correct marshalling technique, and avoiding unnecessary data conversions will often prove beneficial. The focus should be on balancing between efficiency and correctness. Choose the best strategy for the specific requirements, but do not compromise accuracy.

Beyond the technical details, consider the broader context of the system's design. Well-designed interfaces minimize the amount of data that needs marshalling. Effective modularization also aids in minimizing marshaling. This approach improves efficiency and simplifies debugging. Strategic structuring of your objects in both the COM component and your .NET application will aid in optimizing the marshalling process. A well-structured system is easier to maintain and debug. Thorough testing of all facets of the integration process must be included in your development cycle. Comprehensive testing helps to proactively identify and address marshalling problems before deployment. Remember, thorough preparation and planning prevent future complications.

Finally, remember that effective marshalling isn't just a technical task; it's an integral part of building robust, reliable applications. Understanding the intricacies of COM and .NET interoperability is crucial for constructing high-performing, maintainable systems. The successful integration of these technologies relies heavily on the efficient management of data. The proper handling of this data is fundamental to the success of the application. Thorough documentation of your marshalling strategies is also crucial for long-term maintainability and collaboration within a team. This comprehensive approach ensures a smoothly running and reliable application. It is also essential for the future expansion and maintenance of your application.

2.3 Error Handling

Effective error handling is paramount when working with COM and .NET interoperability. Ignoring potential issues can lead to application crashes, data corruption, and a frustrating user experience. Robust error handling, however, ensures a more resilient and user-friendly application. This chapter focuses on practical strategies for anticipating and managing errors that can arise during COM/.NET interaction, making your applications more stable and reliable.

Understanding the potential failure points is the first step towards robust error handling. COM calls, particularly across application boundaries, are inherently susceptible to various problems. These range from simple issues like a component not being registered correctly to more complex scenarios such as network connectivity failures or resource exhaustion. Anticipating these scenarios is key to crafting effective error handling mechanisms.

Proper exception handling is crucial in .NET applications consuming COM components. The try...catch block is your primary tool. Enclose your COM calls within a try block and use catch blocks to handle specific exceptions, such as COMException, ExternalException, or more generic ones like Exception. Don't just catch the exception; log it with details such as the error message, stack trace, and relevant context. This detailed logging is invaluable during debugging and for understanding the root cause of errors in a production environment. Consider using a centralized logging system for better organization and easier analysis.

Early binding, while offering compile-time type checking and better performance, can sometimes mask exceptions. Late binding, though less efficient, offers a more flexible approach and can be particularly helpful in dynamically handling unexpected errors. When working with late binding, always check the return value of COM methods. A non-zero HRESULT indicates an error, and you should handle it appropriately. Mapping HRESULT values to meaningful error messages for the user provides a far more positive experience.

Sometimes, errors aren't directly caused by COM interaction but stem from external dependencies or resource constraints. These might include network issues, database errors, or insufficient memory. Your error handling shouldn't be limited to COM exceptions. You should implement comprehensive error handling to catch and gracefully handle problems at all levels of your application.

By handling these issues with appropriate messages and actions, you ensure your application maintains stability even under duress.

Marshaling errors, though less frequent, can be particularly challenging to debug. Problems in converting data between managed and unmanaged code can lead to unexpected behavior. Careful attention to data types and using appropriate marshaling techniques is vital. Regular testing with different data sets is essential in identifying and resolving these subtle issues.

Beyond simple exception handling, implementing more advanced strategies can significantly improve the robustness of your application. These include retry mechanisms for transient errors, circuit breakers to prevent cascading failures, and fallback mechanisms to provide alternative solutions when primary components fail. These techniques require careful consideration of the specific context and potential failure modes of your application. For instance, a retry mechanism might be suitable for temporary network glitches, while a circuit breaker is more appropriate for persistent component failures.

Testing is the cornerstone of robust error handling. Thorough unit and integration testing are crucial to expose vulnerabilities and ensure proper exception handling. Use test-driven development (TDD) to proactively design your error handling logic, creating unit tests to cover a range of failure scenarios, including boundary conditions and edge cases. Simulation of network failures and other external factors is essential for realistic testing. Remember, a single missed edge case can bring your application to its knees, and thorough testing is the best way to anticipate and address these scenarios.

Documenting your error handling strategy is just as important as implementing it. Comprehensive documentation not only helps you understand and maintain your code but also assists others working on the project. Include details of the expected exceptions, how they are handled, and the logging mechanisms used. Clearly documented error handling makes troubleshooting and future development far more manageable and less time-consuming. Remember, well-documented code is easier to maintain and understand, leading to a more stable and reliable application.

In conclusion, robust error handling is not just a good practice; it's a necessity for any COM and .NET application aiming for stability and user-friendliness. By thoughtfully anticipating potential failures, implementing comprehensive exception handling, utilizing advanced error management techniques, and thoroughly testing your application, you can significantly improve its reliability and create a more positive user experience. This approach is not merely about avoiding crashes; it is about building applications that gracefully handle errors and maintain operation even under unexpected circumstances. Remember to log every error accurately and concisely, making debugging more efficient and allowing for faster issue resolution. This investment in error handling significantly reduces the cost of post-release maintenance and enhances the overall quality and reputation of your software.

3 Building COM Components

Creating a robust COM component requires careful planning. Start by defining its purpose precisely; what problem will it solve? Identify the functionality needed, breaking it down into smaller, manageable units. This granular approach makes development, testing, and maintenance far easier. Think about potential future expansions; a well-designed component can adapt to changing requirements with minimal disruption. Consider using a design pattern, like the Strategy or Factory patterns, to add flexibility and maintainability. This proactive approach will save you headaches down the line.

Interface design is paramount. Each interface should represent a cohesive set of related functionalities. Avoid creating overly large interfaces; smaller, focused interfaces are easier to understand and maintain. Clearly define the methods within each interface, using descriptive names and providing comprehensive documentation. This will drastically improve collaboration and code understanding, especially when working in a team. Remember, a well-documented interface is the cornerstone of successful COM component development.

Next, the implementation phase. This involves writing the actual code that brings your interfaces to life. Use clear, concise code, employing best practices for error handling and resource management. Careful attention to memory management is crucial in COM to prevent leaks and crashes. Regularly test your code to catch bugs early. Unit testing is indispensable. Each method and functionality should undergo rigorous testing to ensure both its correctness and its robustness in various scenarios. This meticulous approach safeguards against costly problems later on.

Registering your component is the bridge between your code and the system. This involves using regsvr32.exe or similar tools to add your component to the Windows registry. The registry stores information about the component, allowing other applications to find and use it. Double-check your registration information to ensure accuracy. A simple typo can prevent your component from being found, leading to frustrating debugging sessions. Moreover, understanding the registry's structure allows for a better grasp of COM's underlying mechanics.

Deployment is the process of making your component available to other applications. Consider different deployment strategies, weighing their pros and cons depending on your application's target audience and its complexity. You may choose a simple copy of the DLL to the target system's directory, or a more complex approach, such as utilizing an installer package to handle dependencies and registry updates automatically. Understanding various deployment methods is essential, given the multifaceted nature of applications. Always thoroughly test your deployment process before a final release.

Thorough testing is an ongoing process, not just a final step. Use a variety of testing methods, including unit tests, integration tests, and system tests, to validate the functionality and stability of your COM component. Use debugging tools effectively to track down any errors that arise during testing. Consider employing different testing methodologies like black box or white box testing to cover a wide range of scenarios. Moreover, remember that testing efficiency is also as important as testing rigorously.

Versioning is a crucial aspect of managing the evolution of your component. Use a versioning scheme, like semantic versioning, to clearly identify updates and changes. Ensure backward compatibility whenever possible, minimizing disruptions for applications already using your component. This is exceptionally important for managing long-term sustainability and reducing user inconvenience. Carefully planned versioning is a testament to well-structured and thoughtful software development practices. Consider implementing a versioning control system to monitor and manage releases.

3.1 Designing COM Objects

Careful planning is crucial for creating robust and maintainable COM objects. Start by clearly defining the object's purpose and the services it will provide. Consider its potential integration with other components, both COM and .NET, anticipating future needs. A well-defined scope prevents unnecessary complexity and promotes reusability. This initial design phase is not just about functionality; it's about establishing a solid foundation for the entire development process. Thorough upfront planning saves you from costly rework later.
Next, you'll need to define the interfaces your COM object will expose. Remember, interfaces are contracts. They specify the methods and properties clients can use to interact with your object. Use a well-defined naming convention to make your interfaces clear and easy to understand. Avoid overly complex interfaces; break down large functionalities into smaller, more manageable units. Well-structured interfaces improve code maintainability and allow for better future extensions. Aim for clarity and consistency in your interface design. This will make your COM objects much easier to use and integrate into larger projects.
Once the interfaces are defined, you'll focus on implementing these interfaces. Each method in your interface will require a corresponding implementation within your COM object. Implement error handling meticulously. Your code should handle all potential exceptions gracefully and provide informative error messages to the client. Using structured exception handling is crucial for creating reliable and robust COM components. In addition, maintain consistent coding style and implement thorough comments throughout your code. This ensures both ease of understanding and maintainability for yourself and others. Remember, clean, well-documented code is easier to debug and adapt in

the future.

Registration is vital for making your COM object accessible to clients. This process involves adding information about your object into the system's registry. This includes details like the object's class ID, interface IDs, and location. Many tools can help you with this process. Consider using tools that automate registration to streamline the deployment process and reduce the likelihood of human error. You can also create installation scripts that ensure seamless integration with your system, regardless of the operating system. Efficient registration minimizes setup issues and improves the overall user experience.

Thorough testing is an indispensable part of COM object development. Use a variety of test cases, including positive and negative tests, to ensure all methods are working correctly and that error handling works as intended. Make sure your testing covers a wide spectrum of possible interactions with the object, simulating real-world scenarios. This will help you identify any unexpected behavior or bugs early in the development cycle, saving time and resources. Employ both automated testing and manual testing to provide comprehensive coverage.

Deployment is the final step in the process. You'll need to package your COM object and make it available to clients. Use a standard installation technology, and make it easy for your users to install and use the object. A good installer clearly communicates steps and provides feedback throughout the installation. Choose an installation package format appropriate for your target users and system. A well-planned deployment minimizes disruption and makes integration into other systems seamless. This ensures the object is available easily and efficiently to those who need it.

Finally, consider versioning. As you develop your COM object further, you may need to introduce new versions. Proper versioning ensures compatibility with older versions while allowing new functionalities to be added. Implement a sensible versioning scheme from the start to prevent compatibility issues. Using a widely accepted versioning system will reduce future compatibility issues and ensure smooth integration. A robust versioning strategy promotes seamless upgrades and prevents conflicts between different versions of the object.

3.2 Implementing Interfaces

The cornerstone of any well-designed COM component is its interface. Interfaces define the contract your component offers to the outside world, dictating what methods and properties other applications can access. Think of it as a carefully crafted agreement; clarity is paramount to prevent misunderstandings and ensure seamless integration. Failing to properly define your interfaces can lead to instability and frustrating debugging sessions later. Precision here is key.

Begin by meticulously outlining the functionality your component will provide. What tasks should it perform? What data will it manipulate? What kind of input will it require? These questions form the foundation for your interface design. You'll want to consider the specific needs of the applications that will use your component, crafting interfaces tailored to their requirements. For example, a component managing user accounts might have separate interfaces for authentication and authorization, promoting modularity and efficient code reuse.

Once you have a clear understanding of the desired functionality, begin defining the actual interface. In COM, interfaces are represented by GUIDs (Globally Unique Identifiers). These GUIDs serve as unique identifiers for each interface, preventing naming conflicts across different components and systems. Tools like the GUID generator in Visual Studio can easily create these identifiers for you, saving you the hassle of manual creation and reducing the risk of errors. Remember, GUID generation is more than a convenience; it's a fundamental step in ensuring compatibility and avoiding naming clashes.

The methods within your interface should be well-named and their purpose self-explanatory. Each method should perform a single, well-defined task, avoiding the creation of overly complex methods that attempt to do too much.

This principle of single responsibility improves code readability, maintainability, and testability. It makes understanding the purpose of each method significantly easier, especially in larger projects, where the sheer volume of code would otherwise obfuscate functionality. A well-defined interface is easier to maintain and less prone to errors. Clearly documented methods are also important; thorough documentation is crucial.

Next, consider the data types used as parameters and return values for your methods. Ensure consistent and efficient use of data types. Avoid unnecessary complexity; choose the data type that most accurately reflects the data being handled. Remember that data may need to be marshalled between processes or different memory spaces, so carefully selecting data types that are easily marshalled can significantly improve performance and reduce errors. For example, simpler data types generally marshal more efficiently than more complex custom objects. Efficiency is not just about speed; it also applies to the ease of understanding and modifying the code.

Finally, testing is crucial. Thoroughly test your interface with a variety of scenarios, focusing on edge cases and potentially problematic situations. This testing phase helps identify any design flaws or unexpected behavior early in the development process, reducing the time and effort spent on debugging later. Remember, effective testing isn't just about finding bugs; it's about building confidence in the robustness and reliability of your component. This confidence will pay dividends when the component is integrated into a larger application. A well-tested interface reduces the likelihood of critical errors in your final application.

Implementing interfaces is more than just writing code; it's about designing a robust, well-defined contract. By carefully planning, implementing and testing your interfaces, you'll not only create more reliable COM components, but also lay the foundation for cleaner, more maintainable, and ultimately more successful .NET integrations. Remember that each method and property is a commitment to your end-user; honoring that commitment through precise implementation is your responsibility. This responsibility extends to your team, too; a well-structured interface benefits everyone involved in the project.

3.3 Registration and Deployment

Successfully registering and deploying your COM components is paramount to their usability. Think of it like publishing a book; the writing is only half the battle. Getting it into readers' hands—or in this case, making your component accessible to .NET applications—requires careful planning and execution. Neglect this stage, and your hard work will remain unseen, its potential unrealized. A well-registered component seamlessly integrates with the system, offering a user-friendly experience. Conversely, a poorly registered one can lead to frustrating errors and system instability, creating a negative impact on your project. The registration process itself involves adding crucial information about your COM component to the Windows registry. This registry acts as a central directory for all installed components, providing the operating system with the necessary details to locate and load them. This information includes the component's class ID (CLSID), interface IDs (IIDs), and the path to the component's DLL file. Tools like Regasm.exe, provided by the .NET framework, automate this complex process, handling the intricacies of registry manipulation, allowing developers to focus on the component's functionality. Without proper registration, the component simply won't be recognized by the system or other applications trying to use it.

Deployment methods vary depending on the complexity of your project. For simple scenarios, copying the component's DLL to a designated system directory might suffice. However, this is often not recommended for production environments, especially when versioning and updating your component are part of the plan. Using an installer package, such as those created with tools like InstallShield or WiX, provides greater control and robustness. Such packages manage not just file deployment but also handle registry entries, dependencies, and other aspects required for a seamless integration. This organized approach helps avoid potential conflicts and ensures smooth operation in diverse environments. Furthermore, installers often provide an easy mechanism for users to remove or update the component, making maintenance much simpler.

Consider the target environment. Are you deploying to a single machine, a network of computers, or a broader range of systems? This significantly influences your deployment strategy. Network deployments often require considerations for security and centralized management. Carefully choosing a deployment method that fits your unique environment is extremely important for the success and integrity of the overall project. Avoid deploying components to shared locations without proper access controls, as it poses security risks. This can cause many issues including the risk of tampering and unauthorized access that compromises system stability. The deployment method you choose impacts more than just ease of use—it's about minimizing potential vulnerabilities.

Thorough testing after deployment is absolutely crucial. Verify that the component registers correctly, loads without errors, and functions as intended within its target application. Use automated tests to ensure consistent performance and to catch any potential regression errors. The most efficient testing procedure includes deploying to a test environment that closely mirrors your intended production setup. This helps to mitigate the risk of encountering unexpected issues only upon deployment to a real-world scenario. Documenting these tests and the solutions to any errors you encounter helps your understanding and your overall performance on the next project.

Remember, the goal is not merely to get your component working, but to ensure it does so reliably and maintainably. Proper registration and deployment go beyond simply making your component accessible; they pave the way for long-term success, streamlining maintenance, upgrades, and future development efforts. Ignoring best practices at this stage can lead to headaches and instability later. Therefore, meticulous planning and adherence to established methodologies are fundamental in ensuring a smooth, successful, and long-lasting integration. A structured and comprehensive approach at this stage benefits you not only in present-time implementation, but also in your overall understanding of the process and future iterations. Consider it an investment in the stability and longevity of your COM component, a vital step towards truly mastering COM and .NET synergy.

3.4 Testing and Debugging

Thorough testing is paramount when building COM components for .NET integration. A robust testing strategy minimizes post-deployment issues and ensures a smooth user experience. Begin with unit testing, focusing on individual methods within your COM objects. This isolated approach helps pinpoint problems quickly, preventing cascading failures. Employ a well-defined test suite covering all aspects of functionality, from simple getters and setters to complex data transformations. Consider using mocking frameworks to simulate dependencies and isolate the component under test, enhancing the accuracy and repeatability of your results. Remember, thorough unit tests form the foundation of your quality assurance process.

Next, move on to integration testing. Here, you'll test the interaction between your COM component and the .NET application that consumes it. This phase identifies issues stemming from interoperability problems, such as data marshalling discrepancies or unexpected exceptions. Use a combination of automated tests and manual exploratory testing to cover various scenarios and potential edge cases. Document your testing process rigorously, including test cases, expected results, and actual outcomes. This detailed documentation simplifies debugging and facilitates future maintenance. Careful planning ensures a comprehensive suite of integration tests, leaving no stone unturned.

Debugging COM components necessitates a different approach than debugging typical .NET applications. The debugging process can be more intricate due to the complexities inherent in inter-process communication and marshaling. Utilize debugging tools such as Visual Studio's debugger, paying close attention to the communication between the COM component and the .NET client. Set breakpoints within both the COM component and the .NET application to track data flow and identify the root cause of errors. Examine the values of variables at critical points in the process to ascertain the source of any discrepancies. Learn to interpret error messages effectively; they often provide valuable clues to help resolve problems more quickly. Remember to thoroughly log all actions and exceptions within your COM component; this can prove invaluable during the debugging process.

Consider using logging extensively. This aids in tracking the component's lifecycle, identifying potential bottlenecks, and pinpointing the source of errors. Implement logging throughout your code, capturing key events, inputs, and outputs. This logging strategy can be invaluable during debugging, allowing you to recreate problematic scenarios and analyze their impact on the system. Strategic placement of log statements, combined with detailed log messages, can significantly improve the speed of problem resolution. Choose an appropriate logging framework to streamline the logging process and ensure consistent formatting of log messages. Use a structured logging approach to further improve searchability and analysis.

Remember, memory leaks represent a common issue in COM development. These can lead to performance degradation and ultimately application crashes. Employ tools like memory profilers to identify and eliminate potential leaks promptly. Pay close attention to object lifetimes and ensure proper release of resources to avoid accumulating unused memory. Be particularly vigilant when working with unmanaged resources within your COM components; using RAII (Resource Acquisition Is Initialization) principles in C++ helps ensure that resources are automatically released. Careful planning and design can prevent many of these types of issues.

Deployment presents another crucial aspect of COM component development. Thorough testing should extend to various deployment environments to identify any compatibility problems or unexpected behavior. Test on different op-

erating systems, versions of .NET Framework, and configurations to increase the chance of catching any potential deployment issues. Ensure that your COM components are properly registered and that all necessary dependencies are included. Automation tools can streamline the deployment process and reduce the risk of human error. Invest the time in rigorous testing, covering various possible deployment scenarios and potential environmental inconsistencies.
Finally, maintain comprehensive documentation throughout the development lifecycle, including the testing phase. Document your test cases, results, and any discovered issues. This comprehensive documentation facilitates future maintenance, debugging, and problem resolution, and is of great value to yourself and other developers who might work on the project later. This can save significant time and resources in the long run. Good documentation is paramount not only to your overall code quality but also to the overall success of your project.

3.5 Versioning Strategies

Effective versioning is crucial for maintaining compatibility and preventing breaking changes in your COM components. Failure to implement a robust versioning strategy can lead to application instability, compatibility issues with existing clients, and significant development headaches. Consider this a vital aspect of creating maintainable and reliable COM components.
Employing a consistent versioning scheme is paramount. Microsoft's recommended approach, using a four-part version number (major.minor.build.revision), provides a granular way to track changes. Increments to the major version signify backward-incompatible changes. Minor version increases indicate added functionality without breaking existing interfaces. Build numbers track internal changes, while revision numbers reflect minor bug fixes. Choosing a clear scheme is a key decision in the development process.
Understanding the impact of each version number change is important.

Altering the major version necessitates updating all client applications that use your component. This requires thorough testing and potentially significant code changes on the client side. Careful planning and communication are essential to minimize disruption. A poorly managed major version increase can trigger a cascade of unexpected problems.

Versioning goes beyond just numbers. Maintain comprehensive documentation for each version release. Clearly articulate the changes, including bug fixes, new features, and any backward-incompatible modifications. This documentation serves as a valuable resource for developers utilizing your COM components, enabling smooth integration and problem-solving. Providing complete details ensures effective use of the component across different projects and versions.

Consider using tools to automate versioning. Many build systems and IDEs provide features for automatically incrementing version numbers and generating version information files. Automation simplifies the process, reducing the risk of manual errors and ensuring consistency across releases. Proper integration into your development workflow is paramount.

Implementing backward compatibility whenever feasible is always beneficial. Design your interfaces in a way that allows for adding new methods or properties without altering existing ones. This means careful consideration of interface design during the initial development phase. Strategies like using optional parameters or adding new interfaces for extended functionality preserve backward compatibility. Forward compatibility might also need attention.

Testing across different versions is an absolute necessity. Before releasing a new version, thoroughly test it with various client applications, potentially across different operating systems and .NET framework versions. This process helps identify compatibility issues and ensures that your components behave as expected in various environments. Regression testing is critical for avoiding unexpected consequences.

Finally, remember that versioning isn't a one-time task. It's an ongoing process that requires careful planning and maintenance throughout the lifecycle of your COM component. Regularly review your versioning strategy and adapt it as needed to reflect the evolving needs of your application and its users. Continuous attention to versioning best practices ensures maintainability. Ignoring versioning leads to a chaotic component landscape.

4 Consuming COM Components in .NET

Accessing the functionality of pre-existing COM components within your .NET applications is a crucial skill. This involves understanding and leveraging two primary mechanisms: early binding and late binding. Early binding, preferred for its performance advantages and compile-time type checking, requires you to have the COM component's type library readily available. This allows the .NET compiler to generate strongly-typed wrappers, ensuring type safety and catching errors during compilation rather than runtime. This approach enhances the reliability and maintainability of your code. You can incorporate type libraries directly into your .NET project using Visual Studio's Add Reference functionality. Simply navigate to the COM tab, select the necessary library, and add it to your project. The compiler will then generate the necessary interop assemblies.

Late binding, on the other hand, offers more flexibility. It's especially useful when working with COM components whose type libraries are unavailable or when dealing with dynamic scenarios. Using late binding, you interact with the COM component through reflection. This allows you to discover and call methods at runtime. The trade-off is that you lose the compile-time type safety that early binding provides, meaning runtime errors are more likely. This method offers dynamic adaptability but comes with a performance overhead compared to early binding. To achieve this, you use the Type.InvokeMember() method or similar techniques to dynamically call methods on the COM object. Proper error handling is paramount in this context.

Type libraries are integral to both early and late binding. They are essentially compiled descriptions of the COM component's interfaces and methods, providing essential metadata for the .NET runtime. They act as a bridge, translating between the native COM representation and the .NET framework's managed code. Accessing this metadata is crucial for effective interoperability. If you're working with early binding, the type library ensures strongly-typed access to the COM object's methods and properties. The compiler uses this information to generate a managed wrapper allowing seamless interaction. This enhances code readability and simplifies development, as you interact with the COM object using familiar .NET constructs. Furthermore, consistent and well-structured type libraries promote maintainability and reduce the risk of runtime errors.

The process of integrating a COM component into your .NET application typically starts with adding a reference to its type library. Once added, Visual Studio generates an interop assembly, a crucial piece that mediates communication. This assembly bridges the gap between the managed world of .NET and the unmanaged world of COM. The interop assembly provides managed wrappers for the COM component's interfaces and methods. You then interact with these wrappers within your .NET code. The advantage of this indirect approach is that your .NET code remains independent from the underlying complexities of COM. This clean separation makes your code easier to understand, maintain, and modify. The interop assembly manages the intricacies of the COM marshalling process, converting data types as needed between the two environments.

Using type libraries is crucial for streamlining the development process. It's like having a blueprint that gives you all the necessary information about the COM component's capabilities. This information enables compile-time checking of your interactions with the component, which means the compiler can catch er-

rors early on, before the application is running, preventing unexpected runtime crashes and behaviors. By adding references to type libraries you can access this information directly, reducing ambiguity and improving maintainability. This structured approach helps to keep your code organized and easily understood. Consider the scenarios where a change is made to the COM component itself. Using a type library will help your code to automatically adapt to such changes, minimizing code modification and testing efforts. This promotes the efficient evolution of both your .NET applications and their underlying COM dependencies. The added benefit, of course, is that using type libraries generally leads to improved performance compared to dynamic approaches.
Finally, always remember thorough testing is essential. After integrating a COM component, rigorously test your .NET application across various scenarios and edge cases. This ensures seamless functionality and identifies any potential issues early in the development process. Careful attention to error handling is also critical, especially in cases of late binding, where exceptions are more likely. Implement robust exception-handling mechanisms to gracefully manage any unexpected errors, preventing application crashes. Incorporating logging into your code will prove invaluable in identifying the source and nature of any problems that might arise. This combination of thorough testing and meticulous error handling significantly enhances the robustness and reliability of your applications. By following these practices, you can greatly improve application stability and user experience, leading to more reliable and predictable software.

4.1 Early and Late Binding

Early binding offers a significant advantage in terms of performance and compile-time type checking. When you use early binding, your .NET application directly references the COM component's type library during compilation. This allows the compiler to verify type compatibility and generate efficient code for method calls, resulting in faster execution speeds. Think of it like having a detailed map before your journey; you know exactly where you're going and how to get there efficiently. However, the downside is inflexibility. Modifications to the COM component require recompilation of your .NET application, potentially disrupting your development workflow. This strong coupling, while beneficial for performance, can become a liability if the underlying COM component undergoes frequent updates. Choosing early binding prioritizes speed and reliability but necessitates a stable and unchanging COM component.

Late binding, on the other hand, provides more flexibility. It involves using reflection to dynamically invoke methods on the COM object at runtime. The .NET application doesn't directly rely on the COM component's type information during compilation, thus allowing you to work with COM components even if their type libraries aren't immediately available or are subject to change. Imagine it as having a compass and navigating by the stars; you're adaptable and can reach your destination even if the terrain changes. You gain flexibility to handle different versions of the COM component without recompilation. The catch is the performance penalty. Runtime reflection is slower than compiled, directly-linked calls, and error handling becomes more critical as type checking is deferred to runtime. The lack of compile-time checks introduces the risk of runtime exceptions if method calls don't match the COM object's capabilities. So, while late binding provides adaptability, it comes at the cost of speed and requires more rigorous error handling during development.

The decision between early and late binding hinges on the specific needs of your project and the nature of your COM component interaction. Consider the frequency of updates to the COM component. If the COM component is static and rarely changes, early binding offers the performance benefits of compile-time type checking and optimal speed. Early binding is the natural choice for scenarios where performance is paramount and the COM component's stability is ensured. For instance, accessing a well-established, rarely-updated system library would greatly benefit from this approach. The increased reliability and performance outweigh the inflexibility.

Conversely, if the COM component is frequently updated or its exact version is unknown at compile time, late binding's flexibility is preferable. Late binding is particularly valuable in scenarios involving third-party components where frequent updates are expected or where dynamic interaction with various versions of the same COM component is required. For example, integrating with a service that might receive updates frequently requires the flexibility of late binding to maintain compatibility without recompiling your entire application. However, careful error handling and comprehensive testing are crucial to mitigate runtime issues caused by the lack of compile-time type safety.

In essence, the choice between early and late binding presents a classic tradeoff between performance and flexibility. Early binding provides speed and compile-time safety at the expense of adaptability, while late binding offers dynamic interaction and flexibility but demands diligent error handling and potentially accepts a performance compromise. A thorough understanding of your application's requirements and the anticipated behavior of the COM component is key to making the right choice. The best approach often depends not just on technical factors but also on the project's overall goals and constraints, considering factors like development time and maintenance overhead. Careful consideration of these factors will lead to a well-informed decision tailored to your specific application's context. Weighing these factors carefully ensures you implement the most suitable binding method for your application, maximizing both efficiency and maintainability. The ultimate goal is to create a robust and efficient application that leverages the power of COM and .NET synergy effectively.

4.2 Using Type Libraries

Type libraries are your best friend when working with COM components in .NET. They provide a structured, strongly-typed way to interact, eliminating the guesswork and runtime errors often associated with late binding. Imagine trying to navigate a complex system without a map; type libraries are that map,

guiding your code safely through the component's methods and properties.
Think of a type library as a detailed blueprint of a COM component. It's an XML-based file containing metadata – a complete description of the component's interfaces, classes, methods, and properties. This metadata allows the .NET compiler to perform compile-time type checking, catching errors before they ever reach runtime. This significantly improves the reliability and maintainability of your applications. It's much easier to find and fix a problem at compile time than chase a mysterious crash during execution.
Using a type library is straightforward. First, you need to add a reference to the library in your .NET project. In Visual Studio, this typically involves right-clicking on your project in the Solution Explorer, selecting "Add Reference," browsing to the type library file (usually a .tlb or .dll file), and clicking "OK." The process might seem minor, but it's the cornerstone of successful COM interop. Once added, you gain access to all the classes and interfaces defined in the type library, ready for use in your code. Your IDE will even provide IntelliSense, giving you code completion and hints as you type, speeding up development and preventing typos.
Let's look at a concrete example. Suppose you have a COM component that provides functionality for image processing. Its type library defines an interface with methods for resizing, rotating, and filtering images. With the type library added, your C\section{code can directly interact with this interface using strongly-typed variables and method calls. This contrasts sharply with late binding, where you would use reflection, incurring performance penalties and increased vulnerability to runtime errors. Strongly typed access via type libraries makes your code far more readable and easier to debug. You'll have clear, precise variable types, enhancing code maintainability.}
Using a type library also offers significant advantages in terms of versioning and compatibility. When a component's type library changes, the compiler can detect these changes during compilation, giving you a heads-up about potential compatibility issues. Early detection is key; it prevents runtime surprises

that can cripple an application. This helps avoid the headaches of deploying applications that silently fail on clients with incompatible versions of the component. Your application will be robust.

Furthermore, type libraries are invaluable for large and complex COM components. The structured information provided by the type library reduces the cognitive load on the developer, making it easier to comprehend the component's functionality and use its features effectively. Working with a complex COM component without a type library is akin to assembling a complex machine without a manual. You'll find the experience significantly less frustrating, leading to faster development cycles and less debugging time with the use of type libraries.

However, be aware of potential issues. Sometimes, a COM component's type library might be poorly designed or incomplete, leading to difficulties in using it within your .NET application. In such scenarios, careful examination of the type library's contents and documentation becomes crucial. Consulting any available documentation is essential, and a good understanding of COM concepts greatly assists in navigating such complexities. Always ensure you're using the correct version of the type library to match your COM component's version; otherwise, compatibility problems might arise. This can potentially lead to a mismatch, causing unpredictable behaviour.

To sum up, type libraries are essential for robust and efficient interaction with COM components within your .NET applications. They are a cornerstone of successful interoperability, promoting strong typing, compile-time error checking, improved version control, and enhanced code readability. While challenges may occur with poorly designed or outdated libraries, the advantages offered by type libraries considerably outweigh the potential drawbacks. You will dramatically improve your efficiency and decrease errors if you employ them. Mastering type libraries unlocks the full potential of COM integration in the .NET framework, enabling you to create reliable and scalable Windows applications. Never underestimate their importance; integrating them into your workflow significantly enhances your development process. Use them effectively. They are an important aspect of the COM/.NET synergy that enhances productivity and reduces development frustrations. Embrace this powerful tool for improved code quality and smoother development cycles. They represent a fundamental improvement for efficiency.

5 Advanced COM Techniques

COM+ significantly enhances the capabilities of standard COM, offering features crucial for building robust and scalable applications. Its integration with .NET opens up a world of possibilities, allowing developers to leverage the power of both frameworks. Consider using COM+'s object pooling to manage the lifetime of your COM objects effectively, reducing the overhead of object creation and destruction, resulting in improved performance, especially under heavy load. Furthermore, just-in-time activation capabilities within COM+ minimize resource consumption by activating components only when needed. This is especially beneficial for components that are not constantly in use.

Security is paramount when integrating COM and .NET. Implementing robust security measures is essential for protecting your application and its data. Leverage the security features offered by COM+ such as role-based security and code access security (CAS). By carefully defining roles and permissions, you can control access to your COM components and the resources they use. Remember that improperly configured security can leave your system vulnerable to attacks. It is crucial to implement the principle of least privilege, granting only the necessary access to each component. Regular security audits and updates to your components are vital to ensure the ongoing security of your application.

Transactions are vital for ensuring data integrity in applications involving multiple components and databases. COM+ provides excellent transaction support through its transaction coordinator. By using COM+ transactions, you can guarantee that all operations within a transaction either succeed completely or fail completely, maintaining consistency in your data. For example, if a multi-step process, perhaps involving several COM objects and database interactions, is wrapped in a COM+ transaction, a failure at any point would cause a rollback to the previous state, preventing partial updates and corrupted data. This feature is invaluable for financial applications or any system requiring absolute data accuracy.

Concurrency control is critical for managing access to shared resources in multithreaded environments. COM+ offers various concurrency management models, including apartment threading and free threading. Selecting the appropriate model depends heavily on the specific requirements of your COM components. For instance, if your components are thread-safe, using the free-threading model can offer significant performance advantages by allowing multiple threads to access the component concurrently. In contrast, if your components aren't thread-safe, the apartment threading model provides a safer, albeit potentially less performant approach. Carefully considering the threading model at design time is crucial for preventing concurrency issues and ensuring stability.

Understanding the intricacies of COM+'s configuration is vital for efficient integration. The Component Services administrative tool allows detailed control over COM+ applications, including object pooling settings, transaction settings, and security configurations. Properly configuring these settings is crucial for optimization and robustness. For example, adjusting the object pool size based on anticipated load can significantly improve performance. Through the Component Services tool, you can fine-tune these settings based on your application's specific demands, balancing resource consumption with responsiveness. Experimentation and monitoring are key to finding the optimal configuration for your specific application.

In practical applications, many developers overlook the importance of thorough testing and error handling when working with COM and .NET. Implementing comprehensive error-handling mechanisms and using structured exception handling to gracefully handle failures within your components is crucial. This is especially important given the possibility of distributed components. A failure in one component can have cascading effects. A robust error-handling approach includes logging detailed error messages to assist in debugging and facilitate troubleshooting in production environments. Employ thorough unit testing and integration testing during the development cycle, to ensure your application functions smoothly even under stress. Don't underestimate the power of well-written log files; they are invaluable when diagnosing issues in deployed applications.

To effectively work with COM components in a .NET environment, familiarity with marshaling is essential. Marshaling is the process of converting data between different memory spaces or process boundaries. Understanding how marshaling works is crucial for ensuring smooth communication between your COM and .NET components. Different data types require specific marshaling techniques. Failure to correctly marshal data can lead to unpredictable behavior, crashes, or data corruption. The .NET framework provides tools and mechanisms to simplify the marshaling process; however, understanding the underlying principles is still essential for troubleshooting and ensuring data integrity.

While early and late binding offer different approaches to interacting with COM components, each has its trade-offs. Early binding, which involves using type libraries, offers better performance and compile-time type checking, reducing runtime errors. However, early binding requires the presence of the type library at compile time and reduces flexibility when dealing with evolving COM interfaces. Late binding, on the other hand, offers greater flexibility, allowing dynamic interaction with COM components even if the type library is unavailable at compile time. The performance overhead associated with late binding, however, is something to consider. The optimal choice between early and late binding depends on the specific needs of your application and the level of control and performance you require. Understanding the difference is crucial when designing your interoperability strategy.

5.1 COM+ and .NET Integration

COM+ extends the capabilities of COM, offering features like just-in-time activation, object pooling, and transactions—all crucial for building scalable and robust applications. Integrating this with .NET unlocks a powerful synergy. Understanding how these technologies work together is vital for experienced developers aiming to create high-performing, enterprise-level software.

The .NET framework provides a managed environment, contrasting with COM's unmanaged nature. This difference requires careful consideration when bridging the two. Data type conversions and memory management are critical factors. Efficient marshalling is essential to avoid performance bottlenecks; failures here can lead to application crashes or significant slowdowns. Remember, proper error handling must anticipate both COM and .NET exceptions.

While .NET offers its own robust features, leveraging existing COM components can be incredibly advantageous. Imagine a scenario where you have a legacy system built on COM—re-writing it entirely would be costly and time-consuming. Integrating it with your new .NET application via COM+ provides a cost-effective solution, allowing you to retain valuable functionality. This approach allows a gradual modernization process, minimizing disruption.

Consider the role of COM+ services. Just-in-time activation is a prime example. Instead of pre-loading components, COM+ loads them only when needed, dramatically improving resource utilization. Object pooling further enhances efficiency by reusing already-created objects, minimizing object creation overhead. This is particularly useful for frequently accessed components, where performance gains are significant.

Transactions are another powerful feature. COM+ provides transactional support, ensuring data integrity across multiple components. If one part of a transaction fails, the entire operation is rolled back, preventing inconsistencies. This robust mechanism is vital for applications handling sensitive data or financial

transactions, ensuring reliability even in case of unexpected errors.
Security is paramount, especially when integrating legacy systems. COM+ provides robust security features, allowing you to control access to your components. This granular control minimizes the risk of unauthorized access, protecting your application and the data it handles. Proper configuration is key to achieving secure integration; consider using role-based security to manage access effectively.
Deployment can sometimes present challenges. Understanding the intricacies of COM+ configuration and the interaction with the .NET runtime is crucial for seamless deployment. Proper registration of components and configuration of COM+ settings are non-negotiable steps. Thorough testing in various environments, from development to production, is essential to uncover and resolve potential deployment issues early on.
Debugging hybrid applications can be more complex than debugging purely .NET or COM applications. Understanding the debugging tools available in both environments is essential. Using tools that allow debugging both the .NET and COM sides of your application is vital for effectively identifying and resolving issues. This might involve using debuggers that can handle both managed and unmanaged code simultaneously. Remember that errors can originate in either the COM component or the .NET wrapper, so a comprehensive debugging strategy is vital.
Choosing between early and late binding in .NET when interacting with COM+ components has significant implications. Early binding provides better type safety and performance at compile time, which reduces runtime overhead. However, late binding offers flexibility, allowing you to interact with components whose type information is not available at compile time. The choice depends on the specific requirements of your application. If you need the performance edge and are sure of the COM component's interface, early binding is recommended. For flexibility, especially with dynamically discovered components, late binding would be a more suitable choice.

Careful planning and design are crucial for successful COM+ and .NET integration. This includes thoroughly understanding the capabilities and limitations of both technologies. Remember to design your components with interoperability in mind, considering factors like data marshalling and error handling from the outset. Thorough testing across the development lifecycle will ensure a stable and high-performing application. This thorough approach minimizes risks and maximizes the benefits of this powerful integration.

5.2 Security Considerations

Security in COM and .NET integration demands careful consideration; a poorly secured system can lead to vulnerabilities exploited by malicious actors. Understanding the potential threats and implementing appropriate safeguards is paramount for robust and reliable applications. This isn't just about protecting your data; it's about maintaining the integrity of your entire system.

Protecting your COM components begins with design. Avoid exposing unnecessary interfaces, limiting the surface area for attack. Implement robust input validation to prevent buffer overflows and other common exploits. Remember, seemingly small oversights can lead to significant security flaws. Never underestimate the power of a well-defined security strategy from the outset. It forms the bedrock for secure development and, ultimately, a more robust application.

.NET offers several security features that can be leveraged to enhance COM interop security. Code Access Security (CAS) allows you to restrict the permissions granted to your COM components. Carefully define the permissions required, granting only the necessary access levels. Avoid granting unnecessary privileges, as this increases potential risks. This granular control empowers developers to create secure applications with minimized attack surfaces. Using strong cryptography for data encryption and decryption during marshaling is essential, especially if sensitive information is exchanged. Always prefer established cryptographic algorithms and libraries, and regularly update them to address vulnerabilities discovered in older versions.

Authentication is another critical aspect. Verify the identity of the COM component you are interacting with, preventing unauthorized access. This can be achieved through various methods, depending on your needs and environment, ranging from simple checks to sophisticated authentication mechanisms using digital certificates or tokens. Ensure that all authentication mechanisms are implemented robustly and securely. Weak authentication opens the door to malicious actors impersonating legitimate components. It is, therefore, a cornerstone of a strong security strategy.

Authorization is equally important; even if a component is authenticated, it needs proper authorization to perform specific actions. Employ role-based access control (RBAC) to restrict access to sensitive data or functions based on the user's or component's role. This principle of least privilege dictates that every entity is granted only the minimum access required to complete its tasks, limiting the impact of a potential compromise. Proper authorization prevents unauthorized modification or disclosure of confidential information.

When deploying COM components, choose a secure deployment strategy. Consider using code signing to establish trust, preventing unauthorized modification. This assures clients that the component is authentic and hasn't been tampered with. Appropriate deployment strategies reduce the risk of malicious code injection and guarantee that your users interact with the intended version of your components. This minimizes the risk of introducing vulnerabilities through compromised installations.

Regular security audits and penetration testing should be part of your development lifecycle. These practices identify potential vulnerabilities before they're exploited. Consider using static and dynamic analysis tools to find and fix security flaws. These measures enhance your security posture. Early detection of vulnerabilities can prevent potentially devastating security breaches. Regular testing makes your applications more resilient and safer.

Always stay updated on the latest security patches and best practices. Security is an ongoing process, not a one-time task. Addressing vulnerabilities promptly reduces your exposure to threats. Consider using vulnerability scanners to check your system for known vulnerabilities and apply the necessary updates as soon as they become available. It's a crucial step in maintaining a robust and secure environment.

Integrating COM and .NET components requires a multi-faceted approach to security. By proactively addressing these considerations throughout the development lifecycle, you can significantly enhance the security of your applications. Remember that security is not just a feature but a fundamental requirement for any robust and reliable system. Never compromise on security; it's an ongoing commitment, demanding constant vigilance and adaptation to new threats. This commitment is crucial for the integrity and trust of your applications.

5.3 Transactions and Concurrency

Efficient transaction management is paramount when integrating COM components within a .NET environment. Transactions, encompassing a series of operations treated as a single unit, ensure data consistency and integrity, even in the face of failures. Without proper transaction management, partial updates or inconsistencies can corrupt data and lead to application instability. Consider a scenario where a financial application transfers funds between two accounts: a successful transaction requires both debiting one and crediting another; failure in either action necessitates a rollback to maintain balance. This is where COM's transactional capabilities, often leveraged through COM+, become crucial for your .NET applications. The seamless integration of COM's robust transaction handling capabilities with .NET ensures that data integrity remains uncompromised. In essence, they function as a safety net, safeguarding against errors and ensuring data consistency within complex operations. Without transactions, you risk data corruption that could have wide-ranging consequences, from financial inconsistencies to program crashes.

Implementing transactions effectively requires a strategic understanding of their scope and the components involved. Transactions are bounded, affecting only specific operations and data. Incorrectly defining transaction boundaries might unintentionally exclude crucial operations, jeopardizing the "all-or-nothing" nature of the transaction. For instance, if you are updating multiple database tables and only one is included in the transaction, partial success—where some data is updated while others are not—becomes a distinct possibility. This might violate data constraints, leading to database inconsistencies and application malfunctions. Therefore, careful consideration must be given to which operations should fall within a transaction's scope. This planning is key to preventing issues that could occur due to poor choices in implementation.

Concurrency, on the other hand, addresses the simultaneous execution of multiple operations or threads. In COM/ .NET applications, you'll encounter scenarios involving numerous threads accessing shared resources, such as database connections or files. Unmanaged concurrency can easily lead to race conditions, deadlocks, and data corruption. Imagine multiple threads attempting to update the same record in a database simultaneously: the last one to write prevails, potentially overwriting critical data from the other transactions. This might lead to inconsistencies and unreliable application results, something no developer wants to happen. Consequently, the careful management of concurrency is crucial to build robust and reliable applications. To mitigate these issues, synchronization mechanisms are necessary to regulate access to shared resources.

.NET provides several synchronization primitives, including mutexes, semaphores, and monitors, to control access and prevent race conditions. However, understanding how these mechanisms interact with COM's threading model is crucial. Improper synchronization can lead to deadlocks, where two or more threads are blocked indefinitely, waiting for each other to release resources. A simple example might include two threads locking two different resources, each thread awaiting the release of the other resource—a classic deadlock. This can stall your application or force its termination. Using techniques like acquiring locks in a specific order or using timeouts to prevent infinite blocking can help you prevent deadlocks from happening. Careful consideration of these factors is paramount to robust application design in this area. Effective synchronization requires careful planning and knowledge of how .NET and COM interact regarding threads.

Employing COM+'s transactional features offers powerful tools for managing both transactions and concurrency. COM+ provides an integrated framework for managing transactions, providing features such as automatic enlistment and distributed transactions. Through COM+, transactions spanning multiple components can be coordinated transparently. In addition, COM+ supports various concurrency models, allowing developers to choose a model appropriate for their application's needs, such as single-threaded apartment (STA) or multi-threaded apartment (MTA) models. Choosing the appropriate model is key to successful synchronization; choosing the wrong model can significantly reduce performance or stability. Using COM+ capabilities, your applications can benefit from the combined power of both efficient transactions and optimized concurrency management for better performance and reliability. It provides a unified solution, thus simplifying the management of complex interactions and promoting reliable application behavior.

For beginners, a practical approach involves starting with simpler transactions and gradually increasing complexity. Begin by defining clear transaction boundaries, encompassing only the operations necessary for a logical unit of work. Utilize .NET's structured exception handling to manage potential exceptions and ensure proper rollback mechanisms are in place. This simple approach ensures that no matter what, the program will maintain consistency and proper functioning. Moreover, progressively introduce concurrency controls, starting with simpler mechanisms like mutexes, before exploring more advanced techniques. Begin by focusing on individual components' functionality, then gradually integrate them into larger systems to optimize performance in complex setups. As you proceed, ensure each stage of development is thoroughly tested to quickly identify and resolve potential concurrency-related issues before deployment.

Remember, transaction management and concurrency control are not independent concepts; they often intertwine within a single application. Therefore, it's essential to consider both aspects during application design. Proper planning is paramount to create a stable and highly performing system that will avoid issues that could arise from bad planning. Failing to properly manage transactions can lead to data inconsistency and system instability; likewise, poor concurrency control can lead to race conditions and deadlocks. Thus, a comprehensive approach, combining the use of COM+ features and .NET's concurrency mechanisms, is crucial for creating robust and reliable COM/.NET applications. Understanding these two concepts allows you to create higher-quality software that will effectively use all the benefits that COM offers.

6 Real-World Application Scenarios

Imagine a financial trading application needing to access legacy market data systems. These systems, often built on older technologies, might expose their functionality through COM interfaces. Your .NET application, responsible for the user interface and modern trading algorithms, can seamlessly integrate with these legacy systems using COM interop. This avoids costly and time-consuming rewrites, allowing you to leverage existing infrastructure while benefiting from the performance and features of .NET. The key lies in understanding how to correctly marshal data between the different environments and handle potential exceptions gracefully. Failing to address these details could lead to data corruption or application crashes. A robust error-handling strategy, involving both COM-specific exception handling and general .NET exception management, is paramount.

Consider a large enterprise resource planning (ERP) system. Such a system may use COM components for specific functionalities like inventory management or order processing. A .NET application could be developed to provide a custom user interface tailored to specific departmental needs. The application would leverage existing COM components within the ERP system to interact with core business logic. This approach avoids reinventing the wheel, ensuring data consistency and reducing development time. However, remember to carefully design the interfaces and consider how to manage concurrency if multiple

.NET applications interact with the same COM components. Efficient resource management is crucial for maintaining system stability.

Let's delve into the world of automation. Many automation systems rely on COM components to control hardware or software devices. Suppose you're building a .NET application to manage a laboratory's automated equipment. This application could use COM to interact with instruments, collect data, and generate reports. The benefit here is standardization; regardless of the specific manufacturer's hardware, your application utilizes consistent COM interfaces. The challenge, however, is in ensuring compatibility across different hardware and software versions, requiring careful versioning and error handling strategies in your COM interactions. Moreover, designing for robust failure recovery within the application is crucial, particularly in sensitive laboratory settings.

Now, think about a content management system (CMS). Existing CMS functionalities often reside within legacy COM components. A .NET application could be created to provide a modern, user-friendly front-end to this system. This would allow the organization to maintain backward compatibility while introducing a more effective interface for content editors and administrators. Effective communication between .NET and COM requires careful attention to data types. Incorrect marshalling can lead to errors or unexpected behavior, hindering the efficiency of the CMS. Thorough testing across various scenarios is essential for ensuring a reliable and stable system.

Finally, envisage a scenario involving a third-party library exposed through COM. This library may offer specialized functionality not readily available in .NET. A .NET application can access this functionality through COM interop, expanding the capabilities of your application without needing to rewrite critical portions of the third-party library. The advantage lies in leveraging existing code and expertise. However, understanding the licensing implications and supporting documentation of this third-party library is critical. It's essential to integrate it securely and reliably, minimizing any potential security risks associated with using external code. Careful consideration should be given to the library's dependencies and potential compatibility issues.

6.1 Case Study 1

Let's imagine a scenario where we need to integrate an existing legacy system written in VB6 with a new .NET application. This legacy system, crucial to the business, handles customer order processing; it's a monolithic application containing vital business logic. Rewriting the entire thing would be expensive and time-consuming, so COM interop offers an elegant solution. We'll design a COM wrapper around the existing VB6 functionality, exposing relevant methods and properties as interfaces. This approach allows the .NET application to interact seamlessly with the legacy system without requiring extensive code refactoring or rewriting. The key is careful planning; understanding exactly which parts of the VB6 application we need to access is crucial for effective wrapper design. We'll need thorough documentation of the VB6 API, identifying the core functions we require for order processing within the new .NET environment. This is critical for creating a functional and efficient interface. Any failure here will ripple throughout the integration process.

The design of the COM component itself needs attention to detail. We'll define clear, concise interfaces, carefully considering data types and error handling. For example, we need to decide how errors are handled and communicated to the .NET client. Should we use standard COM error codes or a custom exception-handling mechanism? Using standard COM error codes improves compatibility, while a custom mechanism offers more granular control, allowing the .NET client to handle specific errors in a customized way. The choice depends on the level of control and error handling complexity needed in our .NET application. We have to ensure both systems have consistent error reporting in case a part fails.

Marshalling data between the VB6 component and the .NET client is a significant step. We will utilize appropriate marshalling techniques to handle data type conversions efficiently, ensuring smooth data flow between the two distinct environments. Understanding how VB6 and .NET handle different data types is critical here. For instance, strings, dates, and custom data structures might require special handling depending on the VB6 implementation details. We'll need to consider both performance and reliability, choosing the right marshalling method to optimize for both. We can't afford slow communication between systems, and data corruption could have disastrous consequences. Choosing the proper marshaling technique depends on how much data is being transferred and the degree of control needed over the transfer process.

Implementing the COM component within VB6 requires meticulous attention to coding best practices. We'll ensure the component adheres to COM standards and guidelines, including correct interface implementation, proper error handling, and effective resource management. It's important to use the correct COM attributes and methods when creating the component. For example, using the correct threading model is crucial for ensuring the stability and reliability of the COM component. This depends on how our .NET application will interact with the component, whether the interaction involves complex calculations or if it simply deals with accessing data. Properly implementing the threading model is essential for avoiding issues of data corruption or deadlocks between the two systems.

The .NET application needs to consume this COM component. This involves adding a reference to the COM library in the project. We can accomplish that by using the "Add Reference" dialog within the .NET IDE, ensuring early or late binding, depending on the needs of the .NET application. Early binding, using type libraries, is often preferred for better performance and compile-time type checking. However, late binding provides greater flexibility for dynamic interaction with COM components, especially if the .NET application might need to work with different versions of the VB6 system in the future. The advantages and disadvantages of early and late binding need to be balanced against the broader project needs.

Deployment of the COM component is an important step. This might involve registering the component using regsvr32 or using a deployment tool to automate the process. Consider that robust error handling during deployment helps prevent problems. The use of a deployment tool is recommended for larger projects since it provides more control over the installation of COM and NET components. The same goes for the deployment of updates to the component.

Testing is essential. We will perform rigorous testing to ensure the integration works correctly under various scenarios. This would include unit testing the COM component and integration testing to check the interactions between the .NET application and the COM component. During testing, logging data is crucial for debugging. This ensures data consistency and provides a record of all interactions between the component and the .NET application. Having all this data can prove invaluable when investigating any failures or performance problems with the legacy system. Such problems, if they exist, can be identified and corrected efficiently thanks to the log data.

Finally, consider future scalability. How will this integration handle increased load and future modifications? The design should accommodate this, ensuring that any expansion doesn't break the interface between the VB6 and .NET parts. We might need to implement mechanisms for efficient resource management, concurrency control, and graceful handling of failures and error conditions. This scalable design ensures future growth in the system and avoids the need for major refactoring or code changes in the future, minimizing the risks and costs associated with future upgrades to the VB6 legacy application. Thorough planning for scalability makes the integration more resilient, versatile, and adaptable.

6.2 Case Study 2

Let's consider a scenario involving a legacy billing system written using COM components. This system, while functional, lacks modern features and a user-friendly interface. Our goal is to integrate it with a new .NET-based customer relationship management (CRM) system. The challenge lies in seamlessly connecting the older, COM-based billing functionality with the newer, more sophisticated CRM without rewriting the entire billing system. This is where the power of COM interoperability comes into play. We can leverage the strengths of both systems.

The first step involves careful analysis of the legacy billing system's COM interfaces. Understanding the available methods and properties is crucial for building a bridge between the two systems. We need to document each interface meticulously, noting the data types used for input and output parameters. This detailed documentation will act as a blueprint for the .NET wrapper we'll create. This wrapper will act as the intermediary, translating requests from the CRM to the COM billing system and vice versa.

Next, we'll create a .NET wrapper class. This class will expose methods mirroring the functionality of the COM components, but using .NET data types. This allows the CRM system to interact with the billing system using familiar .NET objects and methods. It simplifies development and maintenance, shielding the CRM from the complexities of COM interfacing. This wrapper will handle the marshalling of data between the two systems – converting .NET data types to COM types and back. We must pay close attention to error handling within the wrapper to ensure robustness.

The CRM system can then seamlessly interact with the billing system through this intermediary. Requests for billing information, invoice generation, or payment processing are sent through the wrapper. The wrapper takes care of the details of COM interaction, and returns the results in a .NET-friendly format. It's a crucial element in ensuring a smooth user experience; problems in this stage can lead to significant delays and complications.

Now, let's delve into error handling. The .NET wrapper must implement comprehensive error handling. Errors originating in the COM billing system must be caught, translated into meaningful .NET exceptions, and relayed to the CRM system. This translation process is crucial for debugging and maintaining the application. Without robust error handling, it is impossible to create a reliable system. Consider logging all exceptions, with timestamps and relevant context, to aid in debugging and maintainability. A thorough logging strategy significantly speeds up the debugging process in the long run.

Another critical consideration is security. Because the .NET application interacts with a legacy COM component, secure communication is vital. This necessitates implementing appropriate security measures to protect sensitive data during the communication between the two systems. It is necessary to consider access control, encryption, and authentication mechanisms to ensure the application is secure and complies with data protection regulations. This may involve configuring specific security settings in both the .NET application and the COM component.

Finally, performance optimization is crucial. Improper handling of COM interaction can lead to performance bottlenecks. Effective use of techniques like early binding and efficient data marshalling can significantly improve the performance of the integrated system. We will also avoid unnecessary conversions between data types to enhance the speed and efficiency of the application. Profiling the integrated system can help to identify and rectify performance bottlenecks. The careful integration of the systems is crucial to avoid performance penalties. This integrated system, showcasing seamless interoperability between COM and .NET, demonstrates the power of combining the strengths of legacy systems and modern technologies. The result? A more efficient, reliable, and user-friendly system, avoiding the cost and complexity of a full system rewrite.

6.3 Case Study 3

This case study centers on a financial application requiring high-speed, reliable data processing. The core functionality, calculating complex financial models, is implemented as a high-performance COM component written in C++. This component leverages optimized numerical libraries for speed, a crucial requirement given the volume of calculations. The user interface, however, is built using a .NET Windows Forms application for its ease of development and rich user experience features. The challenge lies in seamlessly integrating the high-speed C++ component with the .NET UI, ensuring smooth data flow and minimal latency.

Early binding was selected for this integration. This decision was made after careful consideration of the performance implications. While late binding offers flexibility, the performance overhead in this scenario, where speed is paramount, would be unacceptable. Therefore, the .NET application uses a generated interop assembly to directly access the C++ COM component's methods. This provides a strong type system with compile-time checks, enhancing the overall reliability and maintainability of the application. Extensive testing was performed to verify the accuracy and performance of the integration.

The data exchange between the COM component and the .NET UI is carefully managed. Large datasets are marshalled efficiently to avoid memory bottlenecks. For instance, instead of directly transferring large arrays, the application uses techniques like passing pointers to memory-mapped files. This allows the COM component and .NET application to access the same data in memory without the overhead of copying large amounts of data. This approach significantly improves performance, especially for repetitive calculations involving extensive data sets. We also implemented robust error handling using exceptions and structured exception handling (SEH) to manage potential issues during the data transfer process and component interactions.

Security considerations played a vital role in this application's design. Since the financial application handles sensitive data, secure communication between the COM component and the .NET UI was essential. We implemented robust access control mechanisms within the COM component, limiting access to its functionality based on user roles and permissions. Furthermore, data encryption was utilized during transmission and storage, safeguarding the integrity and confidentiality of financial data. Regular security audits were conducted to identify and address potential vulnerabilities.

Performance optimization was another critical aspect. Profiling tools were used extensively to pinpoint performance bottlenecks. The C++ component's code was optimized to maximize its efficiency, and efficient data structures were employed. The .NET UI was also optimized by using asynchronous programming, allowing it to respond smoothly even during computationally intensive tasks. The application's responsiveness was a top priority, and numerous strategies, ranging from background threads to optimized data transfer techniques, were utilized to achieve the desired performance.

Deployment of the application was streamlined using Windows Installer technology. This allowed for easy and reliable installation on different target machines. The installer handled the registration of the COM component and ensured that all necessary dependencies were correctly installed. This simplified the deployment process, reducing potential issues associated with manual component registration and configuration. Post-deployment, the application monitors its performance and logs errors for enhanced maintenance.

Troubleshooting and debugging the integrated system proved significantly easier thanks to the use of structured exception handling and comprehensive logging. This allowed developers to easily identify the source of any issues that arose during the application's development and deployment. The clear separation of concerns between the data processing layer (C++) and the UI layer (.NET) facilitated debugging and improved the overall maintainability of the system.

This financial application successfully demonstrates the synergy between COM and .NET. The high-performance C++ COM component provides the computational muscle, while the .NET UI delivers a user-friendly interface. Careful consideration of data marshalling, security, and performance optimization, along with a robust deployment strategy, resulted in a reliable and efficient application. The successful integration showcased the value of leveraging the strengths of both technologies to create a powerful solution. The project's success validates the effectiveness of early binding for performance-critical applications and highlights the importance of meticulous planning, comprehensive testing, and robust error handling in such integrated systems. Each step, from design and development to deployment and maintenance, was carefully considered and documented, reflecting best practices in software development. This approach yielded a stable, highly performant application that met its rigorous requirements.

6.4 Case Study 4

This case study focuses on integrating a legacy COM-based inventory management system with a new .NET-based point-of-sale (POS) application. The legacy system, written in Visual Basic 6, uses COM for its core functionality, including database interaction and order processing. The new POS system, however, requires a modern, scalable architecture. The challenge lies in seamlessly integrating these disparate technologies without rewriting the entire inventory system, a costly and time-consuming undertaking. Our approach prioritized leveraging existing functionality while ensuring a robust and efficient integration.

The first step involved a thorough analysis of the COM interfaces exposed by the inventory management system. This crucial step identified the specific methods and properties necessary for interaction with the POS application. We used OLE/COM Object Viewer to examine the type library of the COM component, documenting all relevant interfaces, methods, and data types. Careful documentation was essential for understanding the existing system's data structures and functionalities, preventing unexpected behaviors and ensuring compatibility. This stage revealed that several methods relied on outdated data structures, leading to minor adjustments in the data marshalling process in the .NET application.

The .NET POS application was then designed to consume the COM components using late binding. This approach was chosen for its flexibility, as it did not require prior knowledge of the COM component's type library at compile time. However, to maximize performance, we also implemented early binding where appropriate, after thoroughly testing and verifying the compatibility of data types between the COM component and the .NET application. Through strategic use of both methods, we minimized performance overheads while retaining the flexibility for future expansion. This hybrid approach provided the optimal balance between performance and development speed.

Data marshalling proved to be a key challenge. The legacy system used custom data structures not directly compatible with .NET's native types. To resolve this, we created custom marshaling routines using interop services to convert data between the COM component's data structures and the equivalent .NET representations. This involved careful consideration of potential data loss or corruption issues, ensuring that the data transformation maintained data integrity throughout the integration process. We created comprehensive unit tests to verify the accuracy of the data marshaling. These tests were meticulously designed to handle a wide array of edge cases, particularly focusing on potential error conditions.

Error handling was paramount. We implemented a robust mechanism for catching and handling COM exceptions within the .NET application. This included logging errors with comprehensive details, such as exception messages, stack traces, and relevant data context, facilitating efficient debugging and problem resolution. The logs included timestamps, allowing for tracing the sequence of events and identifying patterns in error occurrences. This comprehensive logging strategy proved invaluable during the testing phase, highlighting several minor inconsistencies in the legacy system's error handling, eventually leading to improvements in both systems' reliability.

Deployment presented unique considerations. The integrated system required careful planning to ensure compatibility across different client machines. This involved meticulous version control and the use of strong-name signing for the .NET assemblies, guaranteeing both security and versioning consistency.

To enhance reliability, we employed a modular approach, separating the integration code into reusable components, reducing the impact of changes and enhancing maintainability. These modules were meticulously documented to provide clear context and facilitate future development and maintenance.
Security was a central consideration throughout the integration process. Access control was implemented to limit access to sensitive data and functionality within the COM component, utilizing role-based security mechanisms to enforce authorization rules. Furthermore, data encryption measures were employed for any sensitive data transferred between the COM component and the .NET application, enhancing the overall security posture of the integrated system. Regular security audits were performed to continuously assess and improve the system's security posture, ensuring the protection of sensitive business data. This comprehensive approach minimized potential vulnerabilities and enhanced the system's overall security profile.
Testing proved crucial for validating the integration's robustness. We employed a combination of unit tests, integration tests, and user acceptance testing (UAT). Unit tests verified individual components' functionalities, while integration tests assessed the interaction between the COM component and the .NET application. Finally, UAT involved real users testing the entire system under realistic conditions. This layered testing strategy allowed us to identify and resolve several unforeseen issues, improving the integrated system's stability and reliability. The iterative testing approach revealed several subtle compatibility issues, leading to refinement of data structures and exception handling within the .NET application.

6.5 Case Study 5

This case study focuses on a scenario where a legacy system, built using COM components, needs to be integrated with a new .NET-based application. The legacy system handles critical financial transactions, processing millions of records daily. Its core functionality resides within several COM objects responsible for data validation, transaction logging, and report generation. A direct rewrite is impractical due to time constraints and the risk of disrupting ongoing operations. Therefore, a phased migration strategy is employed, leveraging COM interop to gradually incorporate the new .NET components while minimizing disruption.

The first phase involves creating .NET wrapper classes around the existing COM components. This simplifies interaction from the .NET side by providing a managed interface, abstracting away the complexities of COM marshalling and reference counting. This carefully designed layer acts as a bridge, translating calls from the modern .NET application to the legacy COM components. Thorough testing at each phase ensured seamless operation and avoided unintended consequences, ensuring the legacy system remains fully functional. The focus remains on incremental change, avoiding potentially destructive large-scale overhauls.

Next, we developed new .NET components to handle specific aspects of the financial transaction processing that required enhancements or modernization. These components interact with the existing COM components via the wrapper layer, gradually replacing older functionalities as deemed necessary. We prioritized areas offering the most significant performance or reliability improvements and also those that were easiest to migrate to a new system to minimize risk. Early deployment of these selective components also allowed for early feedback, helping the whole system development process to iterate and improve.

Data migration was a carefully planned stage. We used a combination of techniques, including custom data transformation utilities and database scripts. This ensured data integrity and consistency throughout the process. We also implemented comprehensive logging mechanisms to track the data transformation and any errors that might have occurred in the process. This made it easy to identify and fix any errors, and was a key step in ensuring data quality and minimizing risks to business operations. The data migration was staged to minimize the time that the system was offline.

Security was a paramount concern. To address potential vulnerabilities introduced by the integration of legacy and modern systems, we employed several strategies. This included thorough code reviews, penetration testing, and rigorous security audits at each stage of the migration. We implemented secure communication protocols and applied appropriate access controls to the COM components and .NET applications, mitigating risks and maintaining compliance with relevant security standards. The use of security best practices is a crucial element to minimize risks associated with this type of system migration.

Finally, a robust monitoring and alerting system was put in place. This system tracked key performance indicators, such as transaction throughput, error rates, and resource utilization. Any deviations from established baselines triggered alerts, facilitating timely intervention and preventing potential disruptions. This proactive approach helped identify and address issues before they affected the business operations. Moreover, it was essential in preventing unexpected failures and reducing the risks to the overall stability of the upgraded system.

The successful integration of the legacy COM components with the new .NET application resulted in a more maintainable, scalable, and secure system. The phased approach minimized disruption to ongoing operations, while the use of wrappers and new .NET components allowed for gradual modernization. The careful planning of data migration and the implementation of a robust monitoring and alerting system ensured the smooth transition to the new architecture. This case study provides a practical example of how effective planning and incremental development can enable successful system integration across disparate technologies. The lessons learned from this project can help in guiding future migration projects, particularly when dealing with legacy systems and the need for maintaining operational integrity.

7 Troubleshooting and Best Practices

Many developers encounter frustrating hurdles when integrating COM and .NET. Understanding common pitfalls is crucial for smooth development. One frequent problem involves mismatched data types between the COM component and the .NET application. Carefully examine the type definitions in both environments to ensure compatibility, meticulously converting data as needed to avoid runtime exceptions. Remember, thorough testing, including boundary condition checks, is paramount.

Another recurring issue is improper handling of COM exceptions. Don't simply catch generic exceptions; utilize specific exception types to diagnose problems accurately. Learn to interpret COM error codes, utilizing tools like the Windows debugger to pinpoint the source of errors within the COM component itself. Proper error logging and reporting mechanisms are essential for effective debugging.

Registry issues can silently cripple your application. Incorrect registration of COM components, due to either manual errors or faulty installation procedures, lead to inexplicable failures. Utilize tools such as regasm.exe correctly and understand its parameters, validating registry entries afterward to verify proper component registration. Regular cleanup of obsolete registry keys is also advisable.

Performance bottlenecks frequently stem from inefficient marshaling. Avoid excessive data transfers across the COM boundary; instead, optimize data structures and consider using techniques like custom marshalling to improve performance. Profile your application to identify performance hotspots and focus your optimization efforts where they'll yield the most significant improvements. Premature optimization is a bad idea, but knowing when to look for ways to improve performance is essential. Efficient memory management is also important; avoid memory leaks by releasing COM objects promptly through proper reference counting and using the correct disposal methods.

Security considerations are often overlooked, yet they're vital. Ensure that the COM components you're using are from trusted sources and follow secure coding practices in both your COM and .NET code. Proper authentication and authorization should be implemented to protect your application from malicious actors. Keep your components updated and patched regularly to mitigate security risks posed by known vulnerabilities.

Early binding, while offering compile-time type checking, can lead to tighter coupling between your .NET code and the COM component. This makes maintaining your system more difficult if the COM component changes or is updated. Therefore, while early binding provides benefits, you might want to use late binding in some instances, depending on how dynamic you need your interaction with COM components to be. Understand this trade-off to make informed design decisions.

Versioning conflicts often cause headaches. Adhere to strict versioning guidelines and use versioning mechanisms correctly to avoid incompatibility problems between different versions of your COM components and .NET applications. Proper testing across different versions is imperative before deploying updates. A robust versioning strategy is not just about numbers; it's about creating a framework for maintaining backwards compatibility whilst also allowing for significant improvements and feature additions.

Finally, remember thorough documentation is critical. Document every step of your COM and .NET integration, detailing component interaction, marshaling strategies, error handling procedures, and any security considerations. Keep your documentation updated to reflect changes and additions. Clear documentation drastically reduces maintenance issues and speeds up debugging. A robust and current documentation helps streamline future development processes.

7.1 Common Issues

One frequent hurdle is mismatched data types between your COM component and the .NET application consuming it. Incorrectly handling variant types, for instance, can lead to runtime errors, data corruption, or unexpected behavior. Always carefully map data types during the interop process, ensuring compatibility between the COM component's IDL (Interface Definition Language) and the corresponding .NET types. Thorough testing with various data sets is essential to uncover subtle type-related issues before deployment. Don't forget to consult the relevant documentation for both COM and .NET to ensure alignment between your data representations. Remember, meticulous attention to detail in this area is crucial for robust and reliable interoperability. Failing to properly manage data types can result in frustrating debugging sessions and potentially serious application failures. Proactive planning and testing are key to preventing these problems.

Another common problem arises from improper registration or deployment of COM components. If a COM component isn't correctly registered in the system registry, your .NET application won't be able to find and use it. This often results in exceptions related to component loading or activation. To prevent this, always utilize the correct tools for registering your COM components – regasm.exe, for example, is a vital tool for .NET developers. Understanding the intricacies of COM registration, including versioning and dependencies, will prevent many headaches. Ensure you thoroughly understand the impact of different registration methods and choose the one that best suits your development process. A simple oversight in registration can lead to significant problems;

therefore, always double-check your registration steps, ensuring the component is accessible to the application. Employing reliable versioning strategies will also aid in the longevity and maintainability of your system.

Security is a paramount concern when working with COM and .NET interop. Improper security configurations can expose your applications to vulnerabilities, potentially leading to system instability or compromise. Pay close attention to access controls, ensuring that only authorized users and applications have access to your COM components. Properly configuring authentication and authorization mechanisms is critical for safeguarding your application's integrity and preventing unauthorized actions. Consult the security documentation for both COM and .NET, and familiarize yourself with secure coding practices for interoperability. Employing appropriate security measures is an ongoing process, not a one-time task. Regularly review and update your security configurations as vulnerabilities are identified and new threats emerge. Proactive measures, including code reviews and security audits, will help you build more resilient and safer systems.

Performance issues often crop up when working with COM interoperability, particularly with large datasets or complex operations. Inefficient marshalling, excessive calls across the interop boundary, or inadequate object lifetime management can severely impact the performance of your applications. Employ profiling tools to pinpoint performance bottlenecks within your code. Optimize data transfer mechanisms, reduce the number of interop calls where possible, and implement appropriate caching strategies to mitigate performance degradation. Effective management of COM objects, and particularly their lifetimes, is crucial for efficient application performance. Remember that optimization is an iterative process, requiring careful profiling and analysis to identify specific areas for improvement. By addressing these potential performance pitfalls, you can significantly enhance the speed and efficiency of your applications.

Finally, handling exceptions gracefully is crucial for creating robust COM and

.NET applications. Unhandled exceptions can lead to unexpected crashes or data corruption, severely impacting the user experience. Implement comprehensive exception handling mechanisms throughout your code, ensuring that errors are handled gracefully and informative error messages are displayed to the user. Design your COM components and .NET applications to handle different types of errors effectively and prevent unanticipated failures. Using proper error codes and messages is crucial, not only to facilitate debugging but also to provide valuable information to the user during unexpected events. Consider incorporating logging mechanisms for tracking and debugging exceptions in production environments. Thorough testing under various conditions and scenarios is essential to uncovering and rectifying potential exception handling issues. A robust strategy for exception handling will considerably improve the reliability and maintainability of your applications.

7.2 Performance Optimization

Performance optimization in COM and .NET integration hinges on understanding the inherent characteristics of both technologies. Unlike purely .NET applications, COM interactions involve marshaling data across process boundaries, a process that can significantly impact speed. Minimizing this overhead is crucial for high-performance applications. Careful consideration of data types passed between COM components and .NET clients is paramount; favoring simpler types reduces marshaling time considerably. For example, using structures instead of complex objects minimizes data transfer, leading to immediate performance gains. This is especially important when dealing with large datasets. Furthermore, efficient memory management is vital, with meticulous attention paid to releasing unneeded COM objects promptly to prevent resource leaks and slowdowns. Failing to do so can lead to gradual performance degradation and ultimately system instability. The timely release of objects minimizes memory footprint, which is especially important for applications handling extensive data or managing numerous COM objects simultaneously.

Proper resource management directly impacts the responsiveness and stability of your application, crucial factors in a satisfying user experience.

Using early binding whenever feasible offers a substantial performance advantage. Early binding, achieved through type libraries, allows the compiler to perform type checking and generate optimized code, enhancing speed considerably compared to the dynamic nature of late binding. This eliminates runtime overhead associated with reflection and type discovery. Early binding ensures that the correct methods are called, avoiding the runtime overhead of looking up methods at runtime. Choosing the correct binding strategy directly affects the application's responsiveness and efficiency. Therefore, for improved performance, favor early binding over late binding whenever the application's structure permits. Remember, optimized code is faster code.

Another critical aspect is efficient interface design. Interfaces should be carefully designed to minimize the number of method calls and the amount of data transmitted. Using aggregations instead of containment, where appropriate, can be an effective way to avoid multiple object instantiations. This reduces overhead associated with creating and destroying objects. Well-designed interfaces minimize communication, resulting in a more performant application. This strategy optimizes interaction between COM components and the .NET client. The emphasis on efficient design choices is paramount to overall application performance. Each decision you make in this phase reverberates through the application's lifecycle.

Consider using COM+ services where suitable. COM+ offers features like just-in-time activation, which significantly improves performance by only activating components when needed. This contrasts sharply with constantly active components that consume unnecessary resources. Leveraging these features directly impacts the overall efficiency and speed of the application. This minimizes resource consumption, resulting in a leaner, faster application. Consider this especially when dealing with long-running processes or applications handling a significant number of concurrently executing operations.

Proper error handling is not just about robustness; it directly influences performance. Efficient exception handling mechanisms minimize the time spent on error recovery. This is particularly crucial for COM interactions which can be prone to errors related to marshaling and component failures. This implies anticipating potential failures in advance and designing mechanisms to catch and handle errors. Failure to do so is not just bad programming; it also slows the application down. Properly designed error handling leads to a significant reduction in the overall execution time.

Finally, thorough testing and profiling are invaluable in identifying performance bottlenecks. Profiling tools allow you to pinpoint specific areas of your code that are consuming excessive resources, allowing you to focus your optimization efforts effectively. This systematic approach offers granular insights into performance issues, guiding improvement strategies effectively. Without such analysis, your efforts might not address the true sources of slowdowns. This allows for targeted adjustments resulting in tangible performance improvements. Testing and profiling are your allies in this final stage of performance optimization. Remember that performance optimization is an iterative process; continuous monitoring and refinement are key to maintaining optimal application speed and stability.

www.ingramcontent.com/pod-product-compliance
Lightning Source LLC
LaVergne TN
LVHW022024200926
848481LV00007B/2535

* 9 7 9 8 3 4 8 4 9 1 9 1 8 *